EDINBURGH CASTLE
PRISONS OF WAR
1781

by
Chris Tabraham
Principal Inspector of Ancient Monuments

On 27 April 1757, the crew of a French ship, the *Chevalier Barte* of Dunkirk, were put ashore at Leith, Edinburgh's seaport, marched up to Edinburgh Castle and locked away in the vaults beneath the great hall. There they remained for the next six years. They were the castle's first prisoners of war (POWs).

Over the course of the next 60 years, thousands more POWs followed in their footsteps, as Great Britain fought across the world to expand its empire. The unfortunate inmates included Americans, Dutch, Germans, Irish, Italians, Poles, Spaniards and French. Most were sailors, caught in action off the British coast.

THIS BOOK TELLS THEIR STORY.

CONTENTS

Background: part of a roll-call of French prisoners recording their receipt of clothes from their home government, June 1781 (courtesy of the Centre Historique des Archives Nationales de France).

DUNGEON

The dungeon beneath the bed-closet in the royal palace at Edinburgh Castle.

Designed by Ramsay Gillies • Principal photography by Mike Brooks• Crown copyright © Historic Scotland 2004
First published by HISTORIC SCOTLAND 2004 • Printed in Scotland from sustainable material by Scotprint, Haddington.
ISBN 1 903570 99 9

At the very heart of the royal palace in Edinburgh Castle is a very special room - the tiny bed-closet where Mary Queen of Scots gave birth to King James VI of Scotland and I of England in 1566. Beneath the floor of that bed-closet lies another special room - a dungeon.

Dungeons, or prisons, were essential elements of a medieval castle, for mighty barons had responsibility for law and order ('pit and gallows') within their barony. Prisons were where miscreants could be held securely pending trial in the baron's great hall. If found guilty, they were sentenced to various forms of punishment, such as paying a fine, losing a hand, or death, sometimes in an unspeakably barbaric way. Given that medieval barons were constantly on the move, prisoners could languish in prison for months, even years, awaiting trial.

The royal castle of Edinburgh was no exception. From the outset of its existence in the twelfth century there would have been a prison. The king delegated responsibility for law and order to his sheriff. He in turn delegated day-to-day responsibility for the prisoners to janitors; the first 'jannie' on record is Reginald in 1175.

The castle's prisoners were a 'mixed bag', ranging from the high-born in society to the lowest of the low. They weren't all kept in the same prison though. The nobility were 'warded', or closely guarded, in rooms in guest apartments, where they were allowed their own servants and luxuries (as long as they paid for them) and a certain amount of freedom within the castle grounds.

'Freemen', such as burgesses and craftsmen, were held in secure prison accommodation elsewhere in the castle, where they had heat, light and sanitation. Serfs, or peasants, were simply thrown into dark holes in the ground, called 'pits', generally devoid of heat, light, air and sanitation.

The dungeon beneath the bed-closet in the royal palace is a good example of a grim medieval 'pit-prison'. Both floors were poky spaces. The upper 'prison' at least had a barred window and latrine closet, whereas the 'pit' beneath had just the cold, hard rock as the floor and a hole in a stone as toilet.

Although we have no record of any inmates, we can picture 'freemen' sitting in their prison thankful only of one thing - that they weren't with the poor souls languishing in the miserable 'pit' beneath their feet.

did you know?

The word 'dungeon' is a corruption of 'donjon', which was the principal, and strongest, tower of a castle where the lord lived. The castle prison was often located in the donjon's basement, so that the lord could keep a close eye on his prisoners!

STATE PRISON

Edinburgh Castle from the Grassmarket

**'While I did in the Castle ly,
In irons close confin'd
For my dear wife and children all,
My heart no ease could find,
To God I did for mercy cry,
As I in fetters lay.
Both night and day to him i'le pray,
Since I am doom'd to die.'**

(from Sergeant William Ainslie's Lamentation and Last Farewell. Ainslie was imprisoned in the castle vaults and subsequently executed for high treason and treachery on Monday 24 December 1716.)

Beneath the great hall in Edinburgh Castle is a labyrinth of stone vaults. From the time they were built around 1480, part of those vaults was reserved for prison use. At exactly that same time, a new prison was added to the Tolbooth, Edinburgh town council's premises beside St Giles' Church in the Royal Mile.

The financier of both buildings was James III (1460-88). James's reign was of momentous significance for Edinburgh, for it was he who declared the town to be Scotland's capital. Responsibility for the new town gaol passed to the town council. No more would the royal castle be used to imprison common criminals; from now on, it would be reserved for those accused of high treason and other 'grite offensis' against the state. In effect, Edinburgh Castle became a state prison.

Ironically, one of the state prisoners warded in the castle was James III himself, in 1482, following an incident at Lauder Bridge, south of Edinburgh, in which he had tried to confront his rebellious nobles, and failed. James was at least saved the indignity of being thrown into his own prison; he was held instead in his own rooms in the palace, where he was watched over by his uncle. James walked free six months later.

Over the next 200 years or so, thousands of men and women accused of 'crymes of treasoun, lese majestie and uther grite offensis' were brought from all corners of the country, and beyond, and imprisoned in the castle. Representatives from almost every aristocratic family and clan can be found in the records.

THE TOLBOOTH (centre) beside St Giles' Church (right) in Edinburgh's Royal Mile.
(After the painting by A. Nasmyth.)

did you know?

A 'tolbooth' was originally a booth in a market place where tolls, or dues, were collected, and where those breaking the market's regulations were detained. In time, it became a proper building, the 'town house', containing the council chamber, a court room and prison. In 1481, part of the old Tolbooth in Edinburgh was 'made a prison'. By 1550, it comprised an 'iron room' (where prisoners condemned to death were held in iron shackles), a 'thieves' hole', and the gaoler's house. It was finally demolished in 1817.

Prison and place of execution

The castle's role as state prison was mirrored by a new, and grisly, role for the Castle Hill (now the Esplanade) - as a place of execution. One of the first to end their days there was Lady Jane Douglas, the earl of Angus's sister, accused of plotting to poison James V and brought to the castle in 1538; her second husband, son and priest were imprisoned with her. Torture on the rack soon extracted confessions, and on 17 July 1538, Lady Jane was led out from the castle, chained to a stake piled around with tarred barrels and oiled faggots, and burned to ashes. Her son and husband were forced to watch from the castle walls. The following morning, her grieving husband threw himself off those same walls, to be dashed to pieces on the rocks below.

Watching burnings, beheadings and hangings was something of a spectator sport in those days. Three years after Lady Jane's cremation, James V himself travelled from Linlithgow especially to witness four clerics being burned for heresy. Over the coming years, Castle Hill made a speciality of burning, beheading and hanging religious dissidents, sorcerers and witches.

Edinburgh Castle and Castle Hill, from Gordon of Rothiemay's plan of 1647. The hangman's gallows is shown standing on Castle Hill, just outside the castle's Spur Battery, awaiting its next victim.

The two new prisons in the castle vaults were like the old dungeon in the palace, except much larger. The upper prisons, capable of holding up to 40 men each, had good-sized fireplaces and windows. The inmates exercised along a narrow stretch of wall-walk outside, long known as 'the Devil's Elbow', though no-one knows why; perhaps the name comes from the tortuous dog-legged route from Crown Square needed to reach the prisons in the old days. (The present route up steps from Dury's Battery was only formed in the nineteenth century.)

At the far west end of the Devil's Elbow were the latrines, projecting out over the castle wall. Below each prison was a 'pit', the dark and dank barely relieved by the narrow slit penetrating the thick wall. A latrine at the head of the steep stone steps was the only creature comfort for the miserable wretches thrown down there.

Latrines

Devil's Elbow

The prisons in Edinburgh Castle as they might have been used around 1530 (David Simon).

Entry from
Crown Square

Great Hall

Upper Prison

Upper Prison

Latrine

'Pit'

'Pit'

11

12   *Covenanters being marched down the West Bow, Edinburgh, from prisons in the Castle and Tolbooth to their place of execution in the Grassmarket (Copyright: City Art Centre: city of Edinburgh Museums and Galleries. Photographed by Antonia Reeve).*

Political prisoners

We can assume that many of those recorded as prisoners in the castle, and not of noble birth, were incarcerated in the castle vaults. They included Farquhar Macintosh and his son, Kenneth Beg ('little Kenneth'), held there in 1502, along with the Milnburn brothers from England. In 1549, two more 'Inglische men', John Forster and Edward Fasart, were being held there as spies. In between, we have the sad record in 1533 of 'a poor man John Muir lang halden [held] in the castle'; his dreadful plight so moved his gaolers that he was given 20 shillings from the privy purse.

The departure of James VI for London in 1603 brought respite from war with England, but the religious and political turmoil that continued to dog Scotland in the seventeenth century provided a constant supply of inmates to the castle prison. They included the marquis of Argyll, incarcerated in 1661 for supporting Oliver Cromwell and subsequently executed, and in the same year ten ministers and a kirk elder, for holding an illegal conventicle (an open-air religious service).

Most prisoners endured their fate; a few tried to escape. In February 1657, Viscount Dupplin and Montgomerie of Eglinton, royalists captured at the Battle of Worcester in 1651 and imprisoned in Edinburgh Castle, managed to escape disguised as coalmen. They were soon followed 'over the wall' by Viscount Kenmore, another royalist. All three were doubtless 'close-warded' in the castle, that is permitted to live in a degree of comfort and allowed a measure of freedom. We have no record of anyone from the lower orders escaping from their miserable pit-prisons.

Archibald Campbell, marquis of Argyll, places the crown of Scotland on the head of King Charles II during the coronation ceremony at Scone, near Perth, in 1651. Ten years later, following captivity in Edinburgh Castle, Argyll lost his own head when he was executed at the Mercat Cross (from the Historie Der Carel Stuart II by Konincklijke Beelteni, Amsterdam, 1660, copyright: The Trustees of the National Library of Scotland).

did you know?

Prison overcrowding is nothing new. In 1607, Edinburgh Castle, according to the Privy Council, was 'so pestered with multitudis of prisoners being commitit thairin for materis of debt and such lyke as no rowme is left to those who aught onlie to be committit to that prisone . . . those guilty of crymes of treasoun, lese majestie and uther grite offensis'.

One of the 'pits' in the castle vaults. The present window is an enlargement of the original slit-window.

Torture most foul

In the 1680s, the country descended further into chaos as the struggle between the Crown and the Covenanters for the nation's soul plumbed new depths of depravity. The notorious 'killing time' saw the castle vaults filled to overflowing - by 1683, no less than 70 members of the landed gentry were in the vaults. For the first time, we read of acts of unspeakable barbarity being inflicted on the inmates, mostly to extract confessions. But no torture can have been more cruel than that meted out to William Spence.

Spence, a former servant of Archibald Campbell, ninth earl of Argyll, the leading Protestant noble, was arrested in London in October 1683, returned to Scotland and put in chains in Edinburgh Castle. Despite repeated interrogation, he steadfastly refused to cooperate, or implicate his former master. In desperation, the authorities ordered that Spence be put 'in the torture' to extract the secret code that Argyll was believed to be using in his letters.

On 25 July 1684, the torturers: 'Re-examined Mr Spence, and booted him, giving him 18 knocks with the mallet upon the wedge, whereas they used to give but six or seven only, and after that charged four soldiers (nay swore them) to continue with him constantly, and to keep him from sleeping, which they did without intermission for 9 or 10 days and nights, when he was ready to die upon the floor for want of sleep. They often pinched him, and touched him with hot things to prevent it & insomuch that he was almost distracted. They threw water upon his broken leg, the balls of his eyes swollen as big as tennis balls. After that they tormented him by the thumbs stretching them towards the same length as his fingers.'

Spence finally cracked on 7 August when threatened with another bout of 'the boot'. He subsequently deciphered two of Argyll's letters from Holland concerning a planned rising in the west of Scotland. For his 'cooperation', Spence was allowed the freedom to hobble about within the castle walls for the next ten years.

The 'boot' – and how to wear it; with associated wedges and mallet

did you know?

Scotland's last recorded torture victim, Henry Neville Payne, was a prisoner in Edinburgh Castle. An English Catholic, captured in August 1690 in the aftermath of the downfall of James VII and II, he was thumbscrewed on both hands and 'booted' for over two hours. He never admitted guilt and was subsequently removed to Dumbarton Castle.

Argyll's 'last sleep'

One of the castle's most famous prisoners was the ninth earl of Argyll himself. He was so appalled by the thought that the Catholic James, Duke of Albany, Charles II's younger brother, might one day become king of Scots that he did all in his power to prevent it. Within a year of James coming to Scotland as Charles's Commissioner in 1681, Argyll was warded in Edinburgh Castle, not once but three times, for failing to acknowledge James's legitimacy to rule. On the third occasion, he escaped, disguised as his step-daughter's elderly servant. He reached Protestant Holland and spent the next four years plotting the downfall of the Stewart dynasty.

In 1685, Argyll returned, hoping to raise a large army from the Covenanting shires. But the failure of his co-conspirator, the Duke of Monmouth, Charles II's illegitimate son, to raise the English in revolt ultimately proved his downfall. He was captured near Paisley, this time dressed as a peasant, and brought again to Edinburgh Castle. He would leave it just once more - for his execution.

Where Argyll was imprisoned on that last occasion is not known, though some say he was confined in the chamber above the Portcullis Gate (rebuilt as the Argyle Tower in 1887). His wife Countess Mary, and Lady Sophie, the step-daughter who had helped him escape in 1681, were already being detained elsewhere in the castle.

The night before his execution at the mercat cross, Argyll apparently dined heartily in his prison cell and then 'slept the placid sleep of infancy'. He went to his death at noon on 30 June 1685, defiant to the last.

'The last sleep of Argyll' by E.M.Ward (1857).
The painting hangs in Edinburgh Castle,
where the ninth earl of Argyll spent his last
night on God's Earth.

'Major' Stede Bonnet, from the same nest of pirates as Walter Kennedy, dangling from the gallows at Charlestown, South Carolina, November 1718. Of his 34 crew, five were Scots, all were hung.

'Black flag' pirates

In February 1720, beside a remote Argyllshire sea loch, 21 suspicious-looking seamen were intercepted abandoning their ship, the *Eagle* and taken into custody. When Campbell of Stonefield, the local laird, went aboard it he was astounded, for there in the hold was a fortune in Portuguese and French gold coin. Campbell had stumbled on some of the most notorious 'black flag' pirates ever to sail the seas.

On 21 May, the pirates, chained and escorted by dragoons, arrived in Edinburgh Castle and were thrown into the castle vaults. There they stayed for the next six months whilst the courts determined their fate. The case was by no means straightforward. Most of the men maintained they were not pirates at all but 'forced men' who had been captured by one of the most infamous pirates of all, Bartholomew 'Black Bart' Roberts, and made to do his dirty work.

Robert Hews, John Clark and the others from the *Eagle* duly stood trial in November. Seven were set free, but the rest were found guilty of piracy and murder and sentenced to death. On 14 December, Hews and Clark, the only ones to admit their guilt, were taken down to Leith Sands and 'hanged by the neck upon the gibbet' until dead; their bodies were then left hanging in chains between the high and low water mark as a warning to others. The rest, proclaiming their innocence to the very last, were hanged in early January 1721.

The pirate captain of the *Eagle*, Walter Kennedy, managed to evade capture and escape to Ireland. Eventually he was betrayed by his lover and hanged at Execution Dock, Wapping, London.

The 'black flag' of 'Captain' Walter Kennedy of the Eagle, most of whose pirate crew, including John Clark, were captured beside Loch Craignish, Argyll, in 1720. Flying the 'black flag' was a crucial act of intimidation deployed at the key psychological moment during an attack.

THE LAST

SPEECH

And Dying Words, of *John Clark*, condemned for Piracy, and executed at *Leith*, December 14, 1720.

I Confess that I was upon the Island of *Providence* when Governor *Rogers* came with the King's Pardon to the Pirates that were there; and that I was one of those who was a pirating before I came into the *Buck-Sloop*: And it is no less true, that when we came out with the *Buck*, we intended to carry on a lawful Trade, but were prevented by the Insurrection of the old Offenders, who took the Sloop away from these that came from *England* in it, of whom *Roger Hughes* was one. It is a great Trouble to me to think of the Suffering of this Man and others that are condemned to die. For alas I was at the Taking of them out of their respective Ships, and forcing them, much against their Wills, to go alongst with us in a very wicked Course of Life. I go out of this World with a heavy Heart, when I think how innocently these Poor Men must suffer. If all those who are taken by Pirates are sentenced to die, a great many of the King's good Subjects will suffer unjustly.

I cannot go out of this World with any Peace of Mind without declaring publickly, that I think they are much wronged and unjustly condemned. Sentence might very justly have passed on the Doctor and me, for he and I were long engaged in these wicked Courses. But as for these poor Men they were taken by us and others from their honest Way of getting Bread, and never did any of these Things they were accused of, but as they were forced to the Working of the Ship, which if they had refused they would have been shot to Death that Moment. It is no Wonder then that they complied so far; for it is natural for us to shun immediate Death, and to preserve our Lives as long as we can. As I am a dying Man, I have told you nothing but the Truth of them.

Further I reckon I am bound in Conscience to inform you, that those poor Men who are now condemn'd, several Times, with the Hazard of their Lives, endeavoured to make their Escape from us; and I declare, on the Word of a dying Man, that I am persuaded, That if Captain *Roberts* had met with them, they would all either have died by his Hand, or at least been set a Shore on some desolate Island.

It

Edinburgh Castle around 1745. A number of leading Jacobites would have been languishing therein as the unknown artist of this painting set up his easel beside Castle Hill.

Ye Jacobites by name

On 15 September 1745, Prince Charles Edward Stewart, or 'Bonnie Prince Charlie' as he is better known, entered the town of Edinburgh and took up court at the Palace of Holyroodhouse. Alas, within the year, his Jacobite army had been crushed at Culloden, and he himself was back in France, fated never to return, far less recover the throne of Great Britain for the Stewarts. ('Jacobite' comes from *Jacobus*, Latin for James - after James VII of Scotland and II of England.)

There had been Jacobite prisoners in the castle from the moment in 1689 when the Jacobite wars began, following the accession of the Protestant King William and Queen Mary to the throne. Sir William Bruce of Kinross, the architect who rebuilt Holyroodhouse for Charles II, wasn't released until 1696.

Many more followed during the 1715 Rising. There was even a 'Great Escape' on 7 August 1716, when 19 prisoners clambered down the rock to freedom; a twentieth fell and was killed. So politically unstable was the situation in Scotland that many prisoners were sent to English gaols as soon as practicable; 18 left the castle for Carlisle on 4 September 1716. A few were left behind, including the unfortunate Macintosh of Borlum who remained in the castle until his death in 1743; he was in his 80th year.

Two years later, the '45 Rising broke out. In the same month that Culloden was fought (April 1746), 43 'common men' were being held in the castle vaults, 19 of whom were 'sick'. But Colonel Guest, the governor, didn't take kindly to commoners defiling his castle and had them sent down to the Tolbooth.

Colonel Guest much preferred to have 'distinguished prisoners', the nobility and ladies. In October 1746, Lady Strathallan with her daughters, Mary and Amelia, together with the Duchess of Perth were there, apparently imprisoned in the same chamber above the Portcullis Gate where Argyll had spent his last night in 1685. They were subsequently joined by Lady Ogilvie, who escaped disguised as her laundress.

Among the last to arrive was Archibald Cameron, Bonnie Prince Charlie's 'aide-de-camp', in March 1753. Having previously escaped to France, he returned to Scotland only to be captured soon afterwards. He was subsequently taken from the castle to London, tried on a charge of high treason and hanged, the last Jacobite to die for the Stewart cause.

Slowly, the castle readjusted to its pre-Jacobite prison role. In 1756, 60 men, newly press-ganged into the navy, were thrown into the vaults for refusing to sail. Two days and nights in the castle vaults were enough to persuade them of the error of their ways and they were soon boarding the sloop *Porcupine*. By now the Seven Years' War with France had started, and impressed men were urgently needed for another war effort.

Two Jacobite prisoners being rounded up by 'redcoats' near Fort Augustus, Inverness-shire, in April 1746, whilst a distraught wife, with child and dog in tow, looks on helpless; painted by Paul Sandby (courtesy of the British Museum).

did you know?

Among the nobility imprisoned after the '45 Rising was James 'Mhor' Macgregor, son of the famous 'Rob Roy'. 'Big Jamie' escaped four days before the date of his execution in 1752, thanks to his daughter, who'd disguised herself as a lame cobbler bringing a pair of newly-soled shoes to the condemned man. A quick clothes change, and Macgregor was soon limping out of the castle gates enveloped in a tattered greatcoat and clutching an old pair of shoes. Two officers were reduced to the ranks, and a warder flogged, for letting Macgregor escape to France.

PRISONS OF WAR

'. . . for the most part miserable holes, fit only for the reception of the worst malefactors. . . dark, long, and narrow, capable of admitting but little light and air'.

(from John Howard's account of the state of the castle vaults in July 1779)

In the late eighteenth century, the vaults of Edinburgh Castle held 1000's of prisoners of war, caught up in Britain's struggle with France, America and their allies.

A contemporary, and satirical, view of the struggle between Great Britain and France in the later eighteenth century (courtesy of the British Museum).

PRISONERS FROM THE SEVEN YEARS' WAR

In April 1757, following a long chase off the east coast of Britain, HMS *Solebay* captured a French ship, the *Chevalier Barte*, off Tynemouth and brought the vessel and her 78 crew into Leith, Edinburgh's seaport. The men were marched up to the castle and locked away. They were the castle's first prisoners of war.

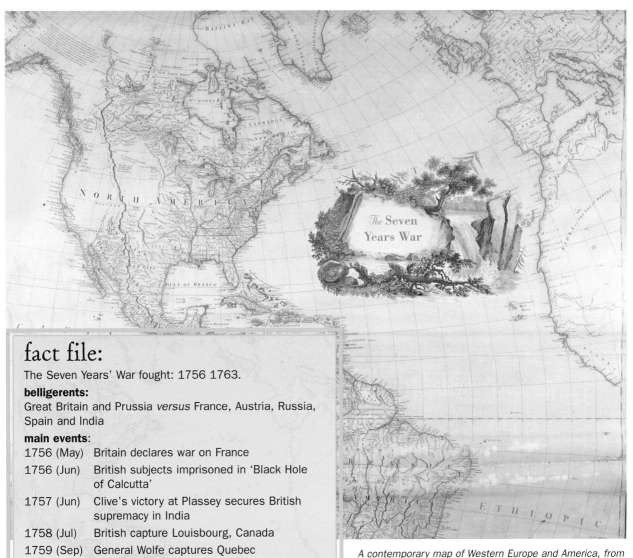

fact file:

The Seven Years' War fought: 1756 1763.

belligerents:
Great Britain and Prussia *versus* France, Austria, Russia, Spain and India

main events:

1756 (May)	Britain declares war on France
1756 (Jun)	British subjects imprisoned in 'Black Hole of Calcutta'
1757 (Jun)	Clive's victory at Plassey secures British supremacy in India
1758 (Jul)	British capture Louisbourg, Canada
1759 (Sep)	General Wolfe captures Quebec
1759 (Nov)	British victory at Quiberon Bay secures naval supremacy
1762	British capture several West Indian islands from France and Spain
1763 (Feb)	Treaty of Paris

A contemporary map of Western Europe and America, from the collection in Trinity House, Leith.

A fireplace in one of the recreated prison vaults. The original grate bears the cypher of George III (1760-1820), the British sovereign who reigned throughout the three wars.

The men of the *Chevalier Barte,* a privateer sailing out of Dunkirk, were probably locked up in the two prisons beneath the great hall lately vacated by those 60 press-ganged men. But where were the hundreds of others who followed after put?

As luck would have it, a new soldiers' barracks, the North Barracks, had been built in 1755 along the north side of Crown Square (where the National War Memorial now stands). During the Jacobite troubles, the castle had been so 'stuffed with men', brought up from the south to patrol the Highland glens and build military roads, that all available barrack accommodation was bursting at the seams. In desperation, the authorities converted part of the castle's labyrinth of vaults into temporary barrack-rooms. Within a year of the last soldier marching out, the first POW was being marched in.

Odd as it may seem, POWs were given better facilities than the soldiers. New fireplaces were installed to take the chill off the dank vaults, and little ventilators fitted 'to extract the foul air'. The prisoners also had an exercise yard, from where they could sell items they had made to folk coming into the castle from the town. Selling wooden boxes and straw hats helped them augment their daily allowance - 6d a day for an ordinary seaman, double that for an officer. Even so they seem to have been in a desperate plight. Of the 362 POWs in the vaults in 1759, 238 had no shirt, 272 no breeches and 331 no shoes. The 'City Hospital for Young Maidens' offered to make shirts for them for 2d each.

HMS ST GEORGE

The POWs included a couple of hundred bedraggled sailors brought from Dundee in October 1759. The sight of them being marched up the High Street, 'many of them about naked', touched those witnessing the scene. 'Those citizens', wrote a correspondent to the *Edinburgh Evening Courant*, 'need no description to move their compassion: their eyes beheld; their hearts asked and some, I am told, could not restrain their tears'. Within days, a fund had been set up by three Edinburgh merchants and the donations flooded in.

Not all Edinburgh folk were moved to such compassion. Indeed, a few suspected that the POWs were abusing the charity offered. A correspondent to the *Courant* told how 'one fellow got yesterday 20 bottles of ale for a suit of cloaths given him by the good people of the town'. The gentleman's cynicism was seemingly borne out when 11 prisoners escaped from the castle in November 1759 - they were 'well clothed in blue, red and cloth coloured jackets, and some wore blue bonnets'.

As the Seven Years' War dragged on, so the numbers of POWs grew. Even though the British and French had agreed a system of prisoner exchange, no actual exchanges from Edinburgh are known, because Scotland was just too far away from the main theatre of war. By the time the Treaty of Paris was signed in 1763, there were around 500 prisoners in the castle. On 2 May 1763, the local paper reported that 'this day the French prisoners confined in the castle . . . were carried to Leith, in two divisions, under strong guards, to be embarked there for France'.

For the next 13 years, the only inhabitants in the grim vaults of Edinburgh Castle were the rats. But with the outbreak of the War of American Independence in 1775, it wasn't long before the next batch of POWs was moving in.

The minute attention to detail by the modellers of the St George, *testifies to one thing – they had plenty of spare time on their hands (copyright: Blair Charitable Trust, Blair Castle, Perthshire).*

Left: The splendid model of the St George, *made by French POWs in Edinburgh Castle in 1760 for the duke of Atholl, and (below) the receipt for £5 4s 6d; both are on display in Edinburgh Castle's Prisons of War exhibition (copyright: Blair Charitable Trust, Blair Castle, Perthshire).*

7th March 1760.

Paid for the St George a 60 Gun Man of War Made by the French prisoners in Edinburgh Castle — 3. 13. 6

for a Box to carry it in — 0. 17. 0

for an Oyl Cloath to keep it Dry — 1. 5. 0

to the Carriage of it to Dunkeld — 0. 9. 0

Total — 5. 4. 6.

'All Europe stands in trembling suspense for the result of the contest in America – France, Spain, Holland and America are praying on the one side; England, Scotland and Ireland on the other.'

The Balance of Power – a satirical sketch of the military position as the War of American Independence reached its climax in early 1781 (courtesy of the British Museum).

PRISONERS FROM THE WAR OF AMERICAN INDEPENDENCE

On 27 June 1781, the 15-strong crew of the American privateer *Newfoundland* were landed at Leith and brought to the castle. Welcoming Hezekiah Welkens, his brother Reuben and the others to their new home were at least 560 French, around 100 Spaniards, maybe 50 Dutch, and an unknown number of 'rebels', that is British and American prisoners. They included the notorious Irishman, Captain Luke Ryan, and at least two of John Paul Jones' men. All were seamen.

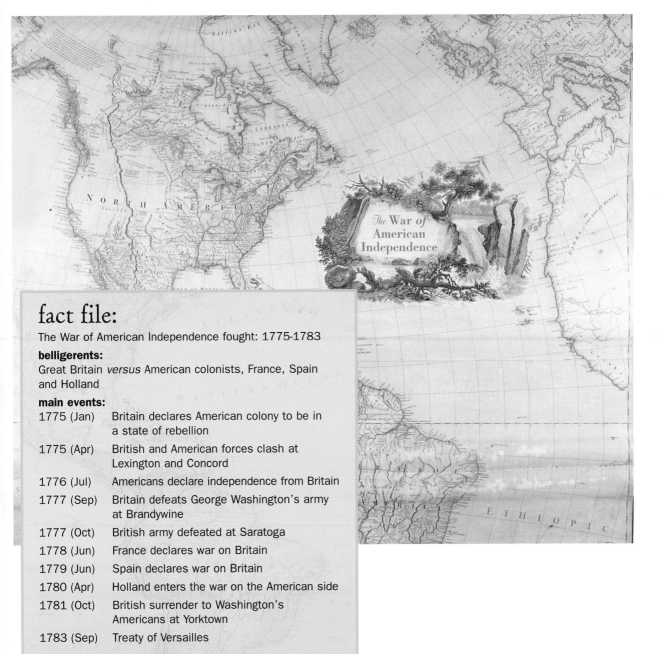

fact file:

The War of American Independence fought: 1775-1783

belligerents:
Great Britain *versus* American colonists, France, Spain and Holland

main events:

1775 (Jan)	Britain declares American colony to be in a state of rebellion
1775 (Apr)	British and American forces clash at Lexington and Concord
1776 (Jul)	Americans declare independence from Britain
1777 (Sep)	Britain defeats George Washington's army at Brandywine
1777 (Oct)	British army defeated at Saratoga
1778 (Jun)	France declares war on Britain
1779 (Jun)	Spain declares war on Britain
1780 (Apr)	Holland enters the war on the American side
1781 (Oct)	British surrender to Washington's Americans at Yorktown
1783 (Sep)	Treaty of Versailles

The crew of the Marquis de la Fayette were on Tuesday and Thursday brought up to the Castle, and the sick carried in carts to the Hospital. They exhibited such a scene of misery and wretchedness as has never before been seen in this country. It seems they had subsisted upon very short allowance since the 3d of May, when they were taken. Many of them died on the passage. The crews of two French ships that were shipwrecked are also landed. These not being considered as prisoners, will be allowed their liberty, upon parole, as soon as they are properly cloathed.

The turnkey's desk in the recreated prisons of war; (inset) a newspaper cutting announcing the arrival of the 140-strong crew of the Marquis de la Fayette to the prisons, 26 June 1781 (courtesy of Edinburgh City Libraries).

But when the cheers of their fellow inmates had died down, the *Newfoundland*'s crew heard a far more disturbing noise - the agonising cries of the 140 crew of the French man-of-war, the *Marquis de la Fayette*, who had arrived just the day before. Theirs had been a dreadful experience. Captured in the West Indies following the sinking of their ship, they'd had to endure a 14-week voyage on scant rations across the Atlantic. When they were eventually landed at Leith on 26 June, they were in a truly appalling state. It comes as no surprise to discover that of the 30 French POWs who died whilst in captivity in Edinburgh during the War of American Independence, 21 were from the *Marquis* alone.

The pitiful sight of the *Marquis*'s crew being escorted up to the castle from Leith that June day moved the hearts of the Edinburgh people, just as the sight of those other French sailors had done in 1759, during the Seven Years' War. Some went straight home, dug up the vegetables from their gardens and brought them to the castle; others gave freely what they could. The captain of the *Marquis*, Le Chevalier de la Neuville, wrote to the *Courant* soon after, expressing his heartfelt thanks: 'The politeness and humanity which the worthy inhabitants of this city have been pleased to show me and my cast-away crew, obliges me to return them my most sincere thanks in your paper'.

The spontaneous reaction of the Edinburgh people says much about the equivocal attitude of Scots to the war in America. On the one hand there was the official line, so movingly expressed in a prayer published in a 1779 issue of the *Courant*:

'Be thou to us, O Lord, a sure guardian and rock of defence, in this time of our necessity, when we are exposed to the dangers and calamities of foreign war. Go forth, we beseech thee, with our fleets and armies; Turn, O Lord, the hearts of our rebellious subjects in America. But spare thy people, O Lord! Spare us.'

On the other was the view articulated by Reverend Nisbet, minister of Eastwood in Renfrewshire, in a letter to his friend, John Witherspoon, the Scots-born Principal of Princeton Presbyterian College who had helped draft the American Declaration of Independence:

'People of fashion and such as would be thought courtiers still say that America might easily have been conquered, but the case is otherwise with the common people, who rejoice in that liberty which they hope to share.'

One Scot personifies this ambiguity perfectly. He also came close to being imprisoned in Edinburgh Castle. His name - John Paul Jones.

'Lord Nord' dangles from a hangman's gallows, 1781 – prison graffiti on a door in the castle vaults.
Lord North was George III's prime minister, whose imposition of swingeing taxes on the American colonies led directly to the War of American Independence.

'Cox-coxcomb! Yield the road,
  or I'll break your bones,
The pi-pirate, trai-traitor comes,
  damn him, Paul Jones.'

PAUL JONES shooting a SAILOR who had attempted to strike his COLOURS in an Engagement.
From the Original Picture by John Collet, in the possession of Carington Bowles.

John Paul Jones – pirate or patriot?

He was born John Paul, at Arbigland on the Solway Coast south of Dumfries, on 6 July 1747, but as a man he terrorised Scotland's coast. He was the son of a humble gardener but grew up to be destined as 'Le Chevalier Paul Jones'. In his day, his very name struck fear and dread into the hearts of his countrymen, but today most Scots claim never to have heard of him. Then he was a 'pirate'; now he is revered as the 'father' of the American Navy and his body lies in state in the Naval Academy Chapel in Annapolis, Maryland, USA.

John Paul Jones was destined for a life on the ocean waves from the time he first smelled the salt air blowing in off the Solway. At the age of 13 he bade farewell to his folks and crossed to Whitehaven, on the Cumberland coast, where he became ship's boy on the brig *Friendship*, then plying its trade to the West Indies and Virginia. His first sight of America was in May 1761, when he visited his big brother, William, who had earlier emigrated to Virginia. Jones fell in love with the country immediately.

Fifteen years later, shortly after the fall-out from the Boston Tea Party, Jones joined the fledgling 'Continental Navy'. In December 1775, he was commissioned first lieutenant, and experienced his first action aboard the *Alfred* during its engagement with HMS *Glasgow*. Two years later, he was terrorising the people of the city of Glasgow itself.

Jones's audacious raid on the earl of Selkirk's home at St Mary's Isle, Kirkcudbright, close to his birthplace, on 23 April 1778, has all the ingredients of a rattlingly good pirate tale - a bold and handsome naval captain (this time aboard the *Ranger*), a beautiful but vulnerable noble lady, and stolen treasure. What possessed Jones to embark on the venture is far from clear, but the outcome, coming hot on the heels of his equally daring night attack on Whitehaven, was obvious enough from the press coverage - widespread panic throughout the land.

The following year (1779), Jones returned, this time putting the fear of God into the people of the Western and Northern Isles and the Scottish east coast. On 14 September, his ship, the 40-gun *Bonhomme Richard*, sailed around the Isle of May and up the Forth towards Leith. Word soon got around - panic ensued.

'You've heard o' Paul Jones, have you not, have you not?
And you've heard o' Paul Jones, have you not?'
How he came to Leith Pier, and fill'd the folks wi' fear,
And he fill'd the folks wi' fear, did he not, did he not?
And he fill'd the folks wi' fear, did he not'

The 'Stars and Stripes' flag flies from the stern of a two-masted vessel – prison graffiti on a door in the castle vaults. The day the flag was adopted by the American Congress – 14 June 1777 – was also the day John Paul Jones received his captain's commission. Jones was the first American to fly the flag in British waters, in 1778.

JOHN PAUL JONES
1747   1792
UNITED STATES NAVY
HE GAVE OUR NAVY ITS EARLIEST TRADITIONS
OF HEROISM AND VICTORY
ERECTED BY THE CONGRESS AD 1912

RANGER   SERAPIS

The final resting place of John Paul Jones, in the chapel crypt at the United States Naval Academy, Annapolis, Maryland (courtesy of the Armel - Leftwich Visitor Center, U.S. Naval Academy).

The unfortunate master of the collier *Friendship* was the first to fall foul of Jones. Thinking the *Bonhomme Richard* to be a British man-of-war, he went aboard her and disclosed how none of the towns on the Forth had guns - they'd all been taken to London after Culloden! The news confirmed Jones in his plan - to take Leith and demand a huge ransom from its 'worshipful mayor and corporation'. As his ships approached, all the people could do was pray for a miracle, among them Reverend Shirra, minister of Kirkcaldy. Gathering his flock on the beach, Shirra turned his eyes heavenward and uttered: 'Now deer Lord, dinna ye think it a shame for ye to send this vile piret to rob our folk 'o Kirkcaldy; for ye ken they're puir enow already, and hae naething to spaire.'

Then, out of the blue, the miracle came. No sooner had the words left the reverend's lips than, in Jones' own words, 'a very severe gale of wind came on, and being directly contrary obliged me to bear away after having in vain endeavoured for sometime to withstand its violence'. That was how close the American Navy got to capturing Scotland's capital city in 1779. As one notable resident, Sir Walter Scott, later recalled, the whole episode hurt his 'pride as a Scotsman' - he was just eight at the time.

Shortly after aborting his Leith escapade, Jones sailed south - and into history - when he captured HMS *Serapis* off Flamborough Head on 23 September 1779. It was his one and only major sea battle, in which he was heard to declare the words which are etched on every American's heart: 'I have not yet begun to fight!'

That single encounter confirmed Jones' reputation as an audacious and cunning naval captain - a reputation that subsequent sad events in a short and lonely life failed to diminish.

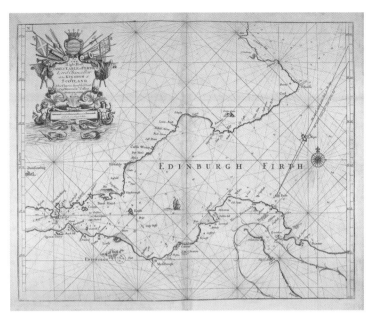

A map of the Firth of Forth (Edinburgh Firth) as charted by Capt Greenvile Collins in the late seventeenth century. John Paul Jones spent three days in the firth before sailing away south to Flamborough Head.
(From the collection at Trinity House Leith.)

did you know?

The wreck of John Paul Jones' flagship *Bonhomme Richard* has recently been found lying in shallow waters off the Filey Sands, in North Yorkshire, not far from Flamborough Head, the site of his greatest sea battle.

EDINBURGH.

A letter from Bridlington, dated Sept. 24. says, " I doubt not but you have heard of the alarming situation we have been in since Tuesday night; but, thank God, as yet we have been only terrified by this Paul Jones. An engagement took place at seven last night, and continued till two this morning, between the Serapis frigate of 44 guns, assisted by the Countess of Scarbrough armed ship of 20 guns, and Paul Jones's ship, the Bonne Homme, of 44 guns, with some smaller vessels, off Flambrough-Head ; and I am sorry to say, that this rascal Jones hath now with him our two ships with their commanders, who distinguished themselves in a most gallant manner. though obliged at last to surrender to superior force, after having made almost a wreck of Jones's own ship. The Serapis had her masts shot away. Several sailors made their escape, and have been examined this afternoon at the Key, but their stories are different as to Jones's loss ; some of them say he had 140 men killed, and his ship quite a wreck. They say, that Jones's plan was to destroy Scarbrough, Bridlington, and Hull, with some other places ; and that he intended landing at Flambrough yesterday morning, but the sea ran too high."

A letter from Scarbrough, dated Sept. 24. says, " On

A newspaper cutting giving an account of John Paul Jones' capture of HMS Serapis, *the Royal Navy's latest frigate, off Flamborough Head, 23 September 1779 (courtesy of Edinburgh City Libraries).*

Ship to shore

The first prisoners locked up in the castle vaults during the War of American Independence were again French sailors, the 35 crew of the privateer *Le Volage*, sent north from Greenwich in November 1778. By April 1779, they had been joined by crews from four more privateers - *L'Audacieuse*, *Le Beauvoisin*, *La Jeune Agathe* and *Les Trois Freres*. These men were probably the 64 POWs, all French, whom John Howard, the prison reformer, found there during his visit of inspection in July that year. In early October, they were joined by 27 Spaniards caught off the west coast by Glasgow privateers.

A two-masted ship carved on to a stone at Dury's Battery in the castle by a bored POW.

Only ordinary seamen were imprisoned in the castle. Their officers, being considered gentlemen, were allowed out on 'parole', that is, permitted to stay in private accommodation on their word of honour and at their own expense. François Le Sable, captain of *Le Beauvoisin*, took lodgings at Dalkeith, where, alas, he died on 30 July 1779.

By then, general alarm was once more spreading along the Scottish coast; 'the infamous Paul Jones' was on the prowl again. The good folk of Dunbar sent an urgent despatch to the *Courant* on 15 September: 'We are all much alarmed at the appearance of a large frigate, French-built, supposed to mount 40 or 50 guns'. Two days later, the paper confirmed that the warship 'nearly opposite to Leith' was indeed the *Bonhomme Richard*, whose 'commander is said to be a Scotsman and to know the coast'.

The port of Leith in the eighteenth century, by an unknown artist. The majority of POWs in Edinburgh Castle arrived at, and departed from, here (from the collection at Trinity House Leith).

Jones' cruise resulted in at least two of his men being imprisoned in the castle vaults. They had been found on one of Jones' prizes, retaken off Lerwick by the *Betty and Becky* and brought to Leith in early October 1779. Jones also had a hand in bringing Dutch POWs into the vaults. Following his celebrated battle with HMS *Serapis* on 23 September, Jones managed to limp into the Texel, the port of Amsterdam, where he was fêted as a hero. When George III was brought the news, he was furious that 'this outlawed desperado' had been so received by a country supposed to be neutral. In his manifesto to the Dutch, declaring that if he didn't receive a satisfactory reply the two countries would be at war, the king included the terse statement: 'In direct and open violation of treaty, they suffered an American pirate to remain several weeks in one of their ports'. Within the month, the first Dutch POWs had joined their comrades in the castle vaults.

The shipping lanes around the British coast were now extremely crowded and dangerous. Had John Howard visited Edinburgh Castle in July 1781 and not July 1779, he would have found not 64 French but as many as 1000 - Americans, Dutch, Irish and Spanish as well as French - crammed into the dark, dank vaults.

did you know?

The authorities clearly anticipated the need for POW accommodation soon after the French entered the war. A letter from the Admiralty to the prison authorities, dated 9 November 1778, gave 'directions for permitting Edinburgh Castle to be appropriated as a place of security for French prisoners, and for your enlarging the windows to the size they were originally of . . .'

The French prisoners' vault in the recreated prisons of war.

Rules and regulations

POWs weren't regarded as ordinary prisoners, nor treated as such. Their presence on British soil was undoubtedly a nuisance, but their conditions were regulated by international law, and monitored as far as was possible by their home governments.

All POWs in Britain were the responsibility of the 'Honourable the Commissioners for taking care of Sick and Wounded Seamen and for Exchanging Prisoners of War', better known as 'The Sick and Hurt'. Their job was 'to see the sick and wounded seamen and prisoners were well cared for, to keep exact amounts of money issued to the receiver, and to disburse in the most husbandly manner'. Samuel Pepys, the London diarist, was a commissioner.

Direct responsibility for the POWs in Edinburgh Castle fell to a local agent, George Middleton. He in turn appointed the 'turnkeys', or prison warders. When the prison was quiet, as in 1779, two or three turnkeys sufficed. But when the prisons were crammed, as in the summer of 1781, soldiers from the garrison helped out.

As soon as a POW entered the castle vaults he was given his bedding – hammock, palliasse (straw-filled mattress), bolster (straw-filled pillow), blanket, coverlet – and a full set of clothes – coat, shirt, breeches, stockings, shoes and cap. He was also given a 'medical' by William Thompson, the surgeon allocated to the castle. A major concern was disease spreading from inmates to the population, a worry that became most acute with the arrival of the bedraggled crew of the *Marquis de la Fayette* in June 1781. Thompson had a house in Edinburgh converted into a temporary hospital for sick prisoners, and during the *Marquis* emergency used another on the city outskirts as an 'isolation hospital'. To reduce the risk of disease, cleanliness in prison was given priority, and the prisoners were required to wash their bedding and clothes frequently.

The food wasn't bad either - it was certainly an improvement on anything common prisoners got, or even the soldiers in the castle for that matter. Each POW received a daily ration of – 2 pints (1100ml) of beer, 1½ pounds (680g) of bread, ¾ pound (340g) of beef, ¼ pint (280ml) of pease every other day OR 1 pound (440g) of cabbage, ¼ pound (110g) of butter and 6 ounces (170g) of cheese instead of beef on Saturdays.

To help make prison life more bearable for POWs, each was given 6d a day. However, there were exceptions. The most glaring anomaly was the unfair treatment meted out to those classified as 'rebels' - the Americans (still regarded as British citizens and therefore not strictly speaking prisoners of war) and Britons (mostly Irish) fighting on the American side. They got just 1 pound (560g) of bread a day and were denied other privileges, such as writing home and prisoner-exchange. Their officers were also denied parole, which is why Luke Ryan, found himself thrust into the vaults along with his 235-strong crew.

The soldiers manning the castle weren't strapping lads - they were all overseas fighting - but members of the Invalids Regiment, the 'Dad's Army' of the day. An advert in the local paper in 1778 instructed: 'Invalid Pensioners residing in Scotland (those who have lost a limb, or are otherwise totally disabled, excepted), to appear personally before the C-in-C of Artillery in Edinburgh Castle, to undergo an examination, that it may be known which of them are capable of doing garrison duty' (courtesy of The Royal Collection © 2004, Her Majesty Queen Elizabeth II).

did you know?

On 30 June 1781, the local paper trumpeted the fact that 'No prisoners of war in any country are better provided for than in Edinburgh, of which Mr Howard, in his very humane treatise on prisons, bears ample testimony'. Perhaps this explains why the Dutch, later that year, 'on hearing of the humane treatment their countrymen in captivity experience in Britain, have ordered all the British POWs in their dominions to be treated with an equal kindness and attention'.

A detail from the 'rebels' vault in the recreated prisons of war, and (inset) an account dated 18 April 1781 of Captain Ryan's capture in the North sea (courtesy of Edinburgh City Libraries).

'Pirate' Ryan

On 18 April 1781, the *Edinburgh Courant* reported that: 'Yesterday morning, about two o' clock, the *Berwick* man-of-war fell in with *Le Calonne*, privateer of Dunkirk, the noted Luke Ryan commander, four miles off St Abb's Head. The *Calonne* struck at half-past eight. Ryan is now in irons. His crew are a mixture of French, Yankies, Scotch, Irish and a solitary Dutchman, who was pilot'. Within hours of his capture, Luke Ryan found himself not on parole in Linlithgow or Dalkeith, but in the same prison as his 235 crew - Edinburgh Castle. So what was it about this man that made him so special?

Ryan, from Port Rush on Ireland's east coast, was a small-time smuggler before the War of American Independence offered him more lucrative employment. He took an American commission to operate as a privateer, and appeared off the west coast of Scotland in September 1779 just as John Paul Jones was leaving the Forth. No sooner had the Scots seen the back of one 'pirate' than another popped up. Ryan announced his presence by bombarding a village on Lismore Island, in Argyll.

Ryan's contribution to the war effort against Britain was immense, far exceeding the damage he personally caused, which amounted to 80 'prizes' and 500 prisoners in the 18 months he terrorised Scotland. Some 40 British frigates had to be withdrawn from the Mediterranean to provide a defensive screen in home waters, resulting in the loss of that area to British control. In Scotland the military had to divert valuable manpower into building shore batteries and raising militias.

Little wonder then that Ryan was treated as a 'pirate' when eventually caught. Flung into the same castle vaults as his men, he spent the next six months attempting to persuade the authorities that he was no ordinary seaman, let alone a 'pirate', and that he had in fact been sailing under the French flag. It made not one jot or tittle of a difference. In early October, he was taken to London for trial - not for treason but for piracy.

Ryan would surely have hanged had it not been for the last-minute intervention of Queen Marie Antoinette, who pleaded with George III to spare his life. Instead, after three years in Newgate Prison, London, Ryan was released and sent to Hampshire. But like John Paul Jones, Ryan was no 'landlubber'. His life spiralled to its close. In 1788, he was declared bankrupt, and in 1789 sent to prison for non-payment of a debt. He died there on 18 June. He was aged just 39.

For the prisoners, life in the cramped castle vaults would not have felt much different from life aboard ship; only the pitch and toss of the sea was missing, and the smell of the salt air.

It also seems, from the evidence we have, that individual crews were kept together, insofar as this was possible. The 93 crew of the *Rohan Soubise*, for example, appear to have fitted neatly into the two medieval prisons entered off the Devil's Elbow, estimated to have been capable of holding around 80 men (just under 1 sq m of floor space per man). And judging by the position of prisoners' names on the various prison rolls surviving in the French archives, shipmates (maybe a gun crew) seem to have been able to keep together in the castle vaults.

Those holed up in the medieval prisons under the great hall continued to use the Devil's Elbow as their exercise yard, and the old toilets jutting out over the castle wall to the south. Those in the western vaults exercised on Dury's Battery - carefully emptied of its guns, of course - and used latrines on the west side newly built for them. During the long hours of darkness in their cells, they used latrine buckets which they 'slopped out' each morning.

Latrines

*Dury's Battery
(Exercise Yard)*

Great Hall
(Barracks)

Pit
('Black Hole')

Devil's Elbow
(Exercise Yard)

The prisons of war in Edinburgh Castle as they might have been used in June 1781 (David Simon).

The Devil's Elbow, with the Great Hall on the left. The two vaults where the 93 crew of the Rohan Soubise were imprisoned were entered directly off the Devil's Elbow, which served as their exercise yard.

The crew of the ROHAN SOUBISE

Of all the POWs, the French seem to have been the best off, for they received a 'royal bounty' from their own government in addition to what they received from their captors. This consisted of an extra 1d a day and clothes - hat, jacket, shirts, breeches, stockings and shoes. The French entrusted the money to London agents and insisted that audited accounts be made of all transactions.

Those records still survive in the French national archives in Paris, and cast a wonderful light on our inmates in Edinburgh Castle.

Each ship's crew is listed separately, starting with its most senior seaman (all officers were paroled elsewhere, of course) and ending with the cabin boys (*mousses*). Each crew member's rank is also given, such as sail master (*maître de voilier*), cooper (*tonnelier*), carpenter (*charpentier*) and ordinary seaman (*matelot*).

The existence of these records, together with the survival in the castle of prison doors covered with graffiti, have provided valuable clues to the POWs' identities - and feelings.

In late April 1781, HMS *Proselyte* and the cutter *Repulse* captured a French man-of-war, the *Rohan Soubise*, in the North Sea after a 13-hour chase. Her crew were landed at Leith shortly after and marched up to the castle.

That much we know from British Admiralty records and newspapers - that and the fact that the *Rohan Soubise* was built in 1780, was initially named *La Comptesse d'Artois*, carried 22 nine-pounder guns, and had sailed from Dunkirk.

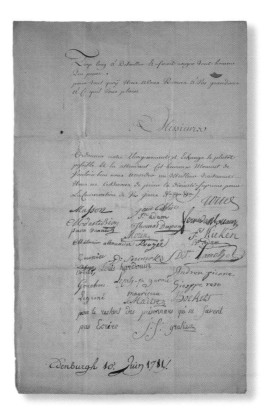

This letter of complaint, dated 10 June 1781, was signed by prisoners from several ships, Including the Rohan Soubise *(note Pierre Garric's name near the bottom). Many more would undoubtedly have signed had they been able to. Instead, Jean Gratiam, of the* Rohan Soubise, *signs on their behalf with the telling words: 'le restant de prisonniers qui ne fasent pas écrire' ('the rest of the prisoners who can't write'). (Courtesy of the National Archives.)*

FOR SALE BY THE CANDLE, 3/6

T Lawfon's Coffeehoufe, Leith, on Thurfday the 19th July 1781, at twelve o'clock,

The French Frigate of War
ROHAN SOUBIZE,

Now in Leith harbour, built in 1780, mounting 22 nine pounder guns, burden 400 tons more or lefs, upon an eafy draught of water, extremely well found in all necessary ftores, and may be fent to fea at a very fmall expence—a moft remarkable faft failor, taken by his Majefty's fhip Profelyte and Repulfe cutter, after a chace of thirteen hours.

Inventories to be had on board, and of Meff. Bell and Rannie, mer-, and James Hamilton, broker, Leith.

An advert from the Edinburgh Evening Courant of 15 July 1781 offering the Rohan Soubise *for sale. The advert had already appeared in previous editions, indicating a lack of interest in the vessel (courtesy of Edinburgh City Libraries).*

48

The name of Peter Garrick (above) and Ducatez (below) carved on a door in the castle vaults. That door (pictured on page 48) also bears the name of Pierre Jean Lefèvre. All three names appear on a list of prisoners (left), dated May 1781, from the Rohan Soubise (and other vessels), recording the receipt of their clothing allowance from the French Government (courtesy of the Centre Historique des Archives Nationales de France).

In the Paris archives we find the flesh to put on these raw bones. Whilst the 16 officers of the *Rohan Soubise* were being escorted to Linlithgow 'on parole', the 93 crew were settling into their new 'home', the two medieval prisons off the Devil's Elbow. We know this was their prison because three of them carved their names legibly into the doors that held them prisoner there.

Pierre Jean Lefèvre, Jean Jacques Ducatez and Peter Garrick all appear on a crew list of the *Rohan Soubise*, dated May 1781, receiving their clothing allowance from the French authorities. Clearly the agent signing on their behalf was British because he couldn't spell their surnames correctly - Lefèvre (on the door) is 'Lefebre' in the records, and Ducatez (on the door) appears as 'Ducattés'. But what was Peter Garrick (the name on the door) doing down in the records as 'Pierre Garric'?

The answer can only be that Peter Garrick, an Irishman judging by his surname, was passing himself off as a Frenchman, successfully it would seem. Whilst he was quite happy to reveal his true identity on the prison door, when it came to answering to his captors he was clearly pretending to be French, thereby avoiding being tagged a 'rebel'. By so doing, he would get his full food ration, qualify for prisoner exchange AND receive his extra 'royal bounty' from King Louis XVI of France.

did you know?

There may be even more to the mysterious Peter Garrick. Not only was a 'Pierre Garric' of the *Rohan Soubise* receiving his extra 1d a day and extra clothes from the king of France; so too was a 'Pierre de Grick' of the *L'Hirondelle*. Could they be one and the same man? If they were, one begins to warm to this Irishman.

The 'rebels' vault in the recreated prisons of war.

Whiling away the hours

So what did the crew of the *Rohan Soubise*, and all the other crews, do to while away their day? Not a lot it seems. Being POWs, they were excused the harsh, mind-numbing punishments routinely meted out to ordinary prisoners, such as working the treadmill, although if any of them broke the prison regulations, he would be sent to one of the pit-prisons for a spot of 'solitary'. Frenchmen called the pit 'le cachot' ('secret hiding-place'); British prisoners contemptuously referred to it as 'the black hole'.

POWs were generally let out of their prison vaults after day-break and left to their own devices until dusk. Most grabbed the chance to get much needed fresh air and stretch their legs in their exercise yard.

The interminable hours of idleness were filled with all manner of activities. Those who could write penned letters home to their families, or to the authorities complaining about their conditions.

Others used their hands to make objects from materials lying about - meat bones, bedding straw and the like. Judging by the exquisite objects they have left behind, they were talented and skilled craftsmen. In addition to items they made for themselves, such as board games and chess sets, their wares were much in demand by others. Every day, between 10 am and 3.30 pm, the people of Edinburgh would come up to the exercise yards and buy tiny wooden snuff-boxes, straw hats and ship models. In return, the POWs could buy luxuries like tobacco.

A tiny needle case made of straw (below left) and an exquisite lady's wooden jewellery box (below), made by POWs in Edinburgh Castle, and now on display in the Prisons of War exhibition (courtesy of the Trustees of the National Museums of Scotland).

Forging a living

Whilst most prisoners put their skills to legitimate use, a few turned to forging banknotes, and with the help of unscrupulous guards managed to pass them into general circulation.

Banknotes then were easy to forge because they had little pictorial delineation and consisted almost entirely of engraved penmanship. The artful prisoners used bones from their rations to make the die stamps and watermarks. A rough print was then made and the details filled in using quill pens.

We have no evidence of forgery going on in the castle during the War of American Independence, but plenty from the Napoleonic Wars. In 1812, an advert in the local press advised readers that forgeries were in circulation, and later that year a forger's 'bone kit' was discovered at Valleyfield POW camp outside Edinburgh; this had been used to forge the 1780 series of Bank of Scotland £1 notes. Around the same time, two forged Commercial Bank of Scotland £1 notes were handed in by duped customers; on the back of one was written: 'This note was taken in the course of business by Alex. Blaikie who wishes he had not taken it'.

Today's banknotes owe their appearance to these early forgeries. Modern banknotes are much more difficult to copy, the paper is specially made, with watermarks and fine metallic security strips woven into it. Some of the printing is fluorescent and glows in ultra-violet light.

One of two forged banknotes on display in Edinburgh Castle's Prisons of War exhibition. The central image is Edinburgh Castle, a place the forger knew well. On the back of the note is written: "22nd Oct 1813. A good note in lieu of this sent to the Rev. Reid Armistead, Whitehaven." (Copyright : Reproduced by kind permission of The Royal Bank of Scotland Group.)

BY ORDER OF THE HON.

The Commissioners for Sick & Wounded Seamen, and for Exchanging Prisoners of War.

THESE are to advertise such persons as shall be willing to contract for a Vessel to carry such Spanish Prisoners as are at Edinburgh and Linlithgow to St Lucar in Spain, and to bring back about 120 Bri-

Courtesy of
Edinburgh City
Libraries.

Homeward bound

An advert placed by the 'Sick and Hurt' in the *Edinburgh Evening Courant* for Monday 23 July 1781 (see inset above) invited ship owners to price for carrying Spanish prisoners to St Lucar in Spain (Sanlucar de Barrameda, near Cadiz, was where Columbus sailed from in 1498) and bring back about 120 British prisoners. The number of Spanish prisoners to be sent would be about 95. We know from subsequent press reports that the *Amity's Friendship* of Leith won the contract, that the vessel sailed in mid August, and duly returned to Leith on 5 December with 90 British POWs.

Thirty-five of those returning Spaniards were very lucky indeed for they had been in the vaults for only two months. They were the crew of the privateer *Santo Christo de Finistre*, of Corcubion in Galicia, who had arrived in the castle on the 30th May. Contrast their circumstances with 27 of their fellow countrymen who had been in the vaults since 6 October 1779 - the best part of two years.

POWs dreamed of being exchanged more in hope than expectation. Weeks turned into months turned into years for many. For those in Edinburgh Castle the possibility of getting onto an exchange list was even more remote, simply because Scotland was too far away

from the main theatre of war, the English Channel and Bay of Biscay. Some inmates even pleaded to be sent south to the crammed prison hulks on the Thames in the belief that thereby lay a quicker route to freedom.

But if the Spanish, French and Dutch POWs felt hard done by, spare a thought for those POWs classified as 'rebels', the Irish and Americans. They weren't even considered for exchange, and had to endure their captivity until after hostilities ceased. John Howard noted during his visit on 27 March 1782, six months after the British surrender at Yorktown, that 15 Americans were still there, plus 'ten who were said to be Irish, who were

closely confined, being out only one hour a day'. By the date of his next visit, in mid August, they had gone. The vaults fell quiet once more.

did you know?

It wasn't just the living POWs who had to wait years to be returned home; so too did the bodies of those dying in captivity. Take poor Clement Seigneuret, for example, a sailor on the ill-fated *Marquis de la Fayette* - he died on 10 July 1781 but his body wasn't returned to his family until five years later.

God save great George our King!

An Old PERFORMER playing on a New INSTRUMENT,
or one of the 42ᵈ Touching the Invincible.

A contemporary Scottish view of the war against Napoleon, showing a soldier from the
Black Watch regiment playing the 'Napoleon' bagpipes. (courtesy of the Trustees of the National Museums of Scotland).

Prisoners from the French Revolutionary and Napoleonic Wars

For ten years and more, the castle vaults lay empty. But when the French executed their king in 1793, Britain and France found themselves at war once more. It wasn't long before French POWs were taking up residence in Edinburgh Castle again.

In 1800, the number was up around the 1000 mark, to the levels reached when the War of American Independence was at its height. By now, the French had been joined by Danes, Germans, Italians and Poles – soldiers as well as sailors.

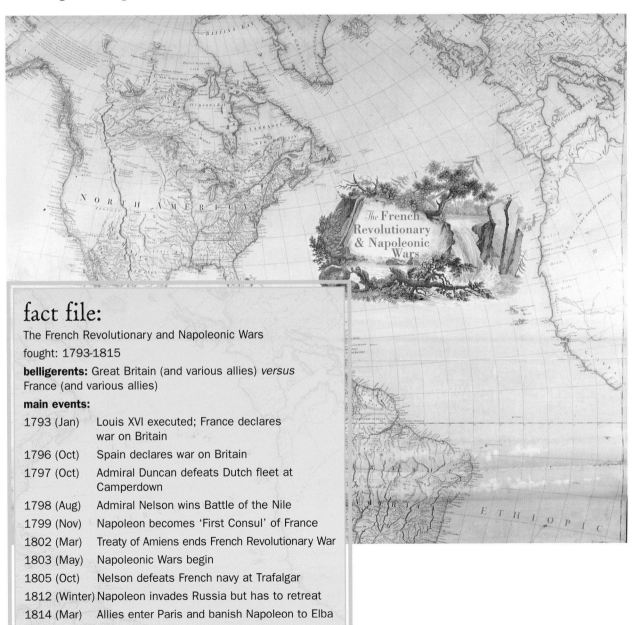

The French Revolutionary & Napoleonic Wars

fact file:

The French Revolutionary and Napoleonic Wars

fought: 1793-1815

belligerents: Great Britain (and various allies) *versus* France (and various allies)

main events:

1793 (Jan)	Louis XVI executed; France declares war on Britain
1796 (Oct)	Spain declares war on Britain
1797 (Oct)	Admiral Duncan defeats Dutch fleet at Camperdown
1798 (Aug)	Admiral Nelson wins Battle of the Nile
1799 (Nov)	Napoleon becomes 'First Consul' of France
1802 (Mar)	Treaty of Amiens ends French Revolutionary War
1803 (May)	Napoleonic Wars begin
1805 (Oct)	Nelson defeats French navy at Trafalgar
1812 (Winter)	Napoleon invades Russia but has to retreat
1814 (Mar)	Allies enter Paris and banish Napoleon to Elba
1815 (Jun)	Napoleon escapes but is finally defeated at Waterloo

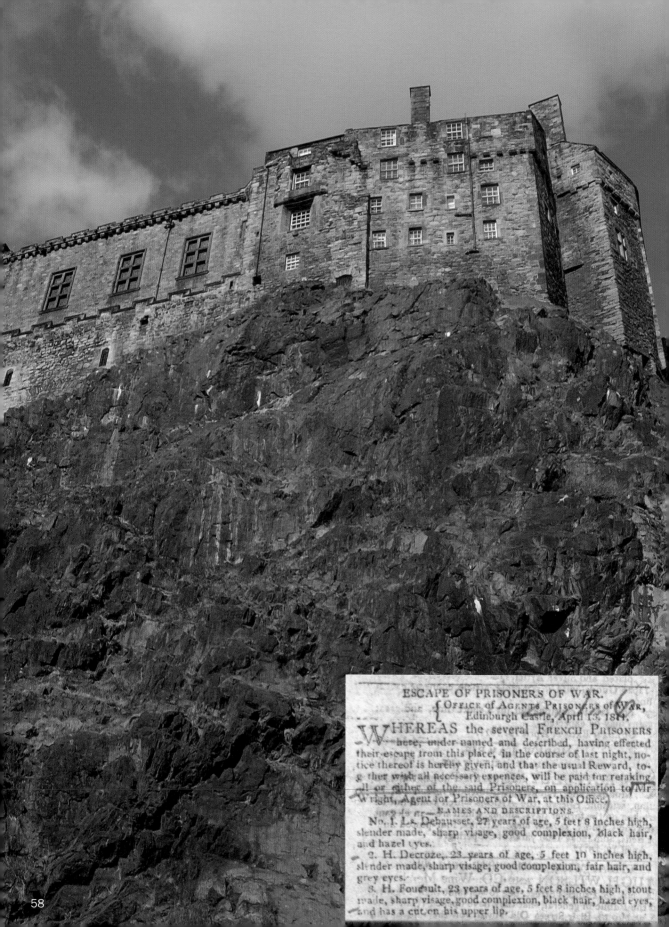

ESCAPE OF PRISONERS OF WAR.

Office of Agents Prisoners of War,
Edinburgh Castle, April 13, 1811.

WHEREAS the several FRENCH PRISONERS here, under-named and described, having effected their escape from this place, in the course of last night, notice thereof is hereby given; and that the usual Reward, together with all necessary expences, will be paid for retaking all or either of the said Prisoners, on application to Mr Wright, Agent for Prisoners of War, at this Office.

NAMES AND DESCRIPTIONS.

No. 1. L. Debausset, 27 years of age, 5 feet 8 inches high, slender made, sharp visage, good complexion, black hair, and hazel eyes.

2. H. Decroze, 23 years of age, 5 feet 10 inches high, slender made, sharp visage, good complexion, fair hair, and grey eyes.

3. H. Foucault, 23 years of age, 5 feet 8 inches high, stout made, sharp visage, good complexion, black hair, hazel eyes, and has a cut on his upper lip.

Over the wall

Every POW dreamed of escape. Many tried, a few succeeded, one or two died in the attempt. We have record of only one escape during the Seven Years' War and none from the War of American Independence. The Napoleonic Wars, however, produced a few memorable ones.

In March 1799, four men escaped. Two broke the conditions of their 'day pass' into the town, and the other two escaped 'over a wall by a rope, having cut a stanchion of a window where they were confined'. They managed to stow away aboard a vessel bound for France. The finger of suspicion fell on Reverend Fitzsimmons, an Episcopalian minister (who happened to be related by marriage to Fletcher Christian, of 'Mutiny on the Bounty' fame). At his trial he confessed to hiding all four in his Canongate residence before persuading a Newhaven fisherman to row them out to Inchkeith Island. He admitted he had felt sorry for 'the poor creatures' and saw his deed not as a crime but as 'an act of common humanity'. He was given three months in Canongate Tolbooth.

Then, in 1811, came the 'Great Escape'. On a dark April night, 49 POWs managed to get out through a hole cut in the parapet wall below 'the Devil's Elbow' and, using their washing-lines, lowered themselves down the south face of the rock. One poor soul lost his hold and fell to his death; the others were all eventually captured and returned to the vaults. The 'hole' is there yet!

Malcolm Wright, the unfortunate agent in charge of the prison at the time, was heavily criticised for failing to comply with 'directions to take from the prisoners every evening the fencing foils [apparently the inmates were allowed to do fencing practice], the various tools they are allowed to use [for making those exquisite objects], and the lines for drying their clothes, in consequence of which the escape of the prisoners was facilitated'.

The mass break-out was the last straw for the prison authorities.

The 'hole' off the Devil's Elbow, through which the 49 intrepid POWs made their 'great escape' in 1811.

Left: The precipitous castle rock below the Devil's Elbow, down which many a POW has clambered in a desperate bid for freedom. This included 49 men on the night of 12 April 1811, whose names and descriptions (see inset) appeared in the following day's local evening paper (courtesy of Edinburgh City Libraries).

The monument at Valleyfield POW camp, near Penicuik, erected in 1830. The inscription, in French and English, reads: 'the mortal remains of 309 prisoners of war, who died 1811-14 in this neighbourhood, are interred near this spot.'

The last prisoners

As the war dragged on, so the numbers continued to rise. Soon other areas of the castle were being pressed into use as prisons. They included the vaults of the New Barracks, which had only been completed in 1799. Its army occupants weren't much pleased with their new tenants because of the possibility of them 'deranging the present garrison and causing danger to the military stores'.

In desperation, the authorities cast around for alternatives, and in 1804, 200 POWs were marched off to Greenlaw, to the south of the city. Still they flooded in. Conditions grew even more unbearable in the vaults. The French and Spanish 'constantly engaged in feuds' and had to be physically separated. The diet also deteriorated - one visitor reported that 'the soup was shockingly bad, apparently like water taken out of a ditch, and no meat nor vegetables of any kind to be seen in it'. Hardly surprising that the inmates were bent on escape.

The 'great escape' of 1811 was the last straw. In December of that year, the Admiralty declared that 'in consequence of the ease with which French prisoners of war can escape from Edinburgh Castle . . . [we are] pleased to direct that this depot be abolished'.

In truth, the decision had been taken before the mass break-out. In 1810, the government had bought the Valleyfield paper mills in Penicuik, south of the city, and turned it into a camp capable of housing 5000 inmates in purpose-built accommodation. With Valleyfield up and running, Edinburgh Castle reverted to being used as a high-security prison - the

'Colditz' of its day (Colditz Castle, near Leipzig, was where the Germans kept equally troublesome British POWs during World War II). The hardened prisoners sent to Edinburgh Castle after 1811 were thrown into the medieval pits, from which there was little prospect of escape.

Fortunately for them the end was not far away. In 1814, following the false dawn that followed the capture of Napoleon, the last remaining inmates in the vaults were escorted to Leith and embarked for France.

Was it coincidence, or did someone in the Transport Office have a sense of history? The ship chosen to take away those last remaining POWs on 15 June was none other than HMS *Solebay*, the self-same vessel that had brought the first POWs to Leith 57 years earlier.

The recent removal of layers of paint from this door in the castle vaults revealed the stencilled letters HOSP[L] and BED[G]. A plan of the castle, dated 1811, confirms that this part of the prison was operating as a hospital and bedding store by this time.

Dury's Battery and the Devil's Elbow, the two prisoners'
exercise yards in Edinburgh Castle, with the Queen Anne
Building towering above them. Arthur's Seat, Edinburgh's
'mountain in the city', lurks in the background.

Other than to house the odd drunken soldier, the castle vaults ceased to be used as prisons after 1814. Until, that is, an extraordinary episode involving an extraordinary man imprisoned there during another war. His name was David Kirkwood, and the war was World War I (1914-18).

Kirkwood was a shop steward at a Glasgow engineering works when the war broke out. Disillusioned with the way things were going, he and others, including John Maclean, formed the Clyde Workers Committee in early 1916. They became known as the 'Red Clydesiders'.

Kirkwood was soon arrested and 'deported' to Edinburgh. By January 1917, though, he was back 'illegally' in Glasgow, and once again he was arrested. This time the authorities took no chances. They returned him to Edinburgh - and locked him up in the castle.

Judging by his own dramatic account, it sounds as if he was thrown into one of the pit-prisons in the castle vaults:

'My new habitation was a vault, far below the ground, into which the only light entered from a small grated window high up near the roof. I was a done man.'

David Kirkwood subsequently became a Labour MP (1922) and a Lord (1947), taking the title Baron Kirkwood of Bearsden. He was also the first Scottish MP to table a Bill for the return of the Stone of Destiny from Westminster to Scotland. Today, that icon of Scottish nationhood lies on display in the Crown Room of Edinburgh Castle - barely 100m from where Kirkwood was held prisoner.

Acknowledgments

HISTORIC SCOTLAND gratefully acknowledges the help of the following individuals and organisations in the production of this book, and the Prisons of War exhibition in Edinburgh Castle:

Bruno Galland and **Phillippe Henrat**, of the Centre Historique des Archives Nationales de France, for making us so welcome.

Eric J Graham, of the Early Scottish Maritime Exchange, for providing valuable insights into piracy, Captain Ryan and so much more besides.

Brian Bath and **Lidia Polubiec**, for their painstaking research, which underpinned the recreation of the Prisons of War in Edinburgh Castle.

Gordon Ewart, of Kirkdale Archaeology, for his company's careful and considered archaeological and standing building recording work in the castle vaults.

David Simon, for his wonderfully evocative reconstruction paintings of the prisons of war.

To find out more

Francis Abell *Prisoners of War in Britain, 1756-1815: a record of their lives, their romance and their sufferings* (Oxford, 1914)

Nick Allen 'The French Prisons in Edinburgh Castle' in *The Book of the Old Edinburgh Club*, vol 35 (1985), 160-70

Joy Cameron *Prisons & Punishment in Scotland from the Middle Ages to the Present* (Edinburgh, 1983)

Eric J Graham *A Maritime History of Scotland 1650-1790* (East Linton, 2002)

John Howard *The State of the Prisons in England and Wales* (Warrington, 1784)

Samuel Eliot Morison *John Paul Jones: A Sailor's Biography* (New York, 1959)

Donald Petrie 'The Piracy Trial of Luke Ryan', *American Neptune*, vol 55, 3 (1995), 185-204

Chris Tabraham *Edinburgh Castle* (Edinburgh, 2004)